NINJAS

石川五右衛門
豊国画

NINJAS

ODYSSEYS

SARA GILBERT

CREATIVE EDUCATION · CREATIVE PAPERBACKS

Published by Creative Education and Creative Paperbacks
P.O. Box 227, Mankato, Minnesota 56002
Creative Education and Creative Paperbacks
are imprints of The Creative Company
www.thecreativecompany.us

Design by Graham Morgan
Art direction by Tom Morgan

Images by Getty Images/filo, 54, Julian Elliott Photography, 61, lisegagne, 8, RichLegg, 42, YS graphic, 62, 1001nights, 18; Microsoft Copilot/46, 67; Unsplash/Corina Rainer, 37; Wikimedia Commons/Chris Gladis, 49, Frederick Sutton Studio, 17, Fujibayashi Yasutake, Fujibayashi Sabuji, 64, Kano School, 11, Kanō Tan'yū, 27, Katsushika Hokusai/AMorozov, 4–5, Kitex2002, 6, Motokoka, 24, public domain, 12, 22, 32–33, 58, 75, raybdbomb, 28, Suzuki Shin'ichi I, 68, Utagawa Kunisada, cover, 2, 50, 70–71, Vanessa Shibata, 57

Library of Congress Cataloging-in-Publication Data
Names: Gilbert, Sara, author.
Title: Ninjas / Sara Gilbert.
Description: Mankato, Minnesota : Creative Education and Creative Paperbacks, [2026] | Series: Odysseys in combat | Includes bibliographical references and index. | Audience: Ages 12–15 years | Audience: Grades 7–9 | Summary: "Prepare for battle alongside the secretive, shadowy warriors of Japan called ninjas by learning about their weapons, combat skills, and reasons for fighting. Includes a glossary, sidebars, index, and further resources"—Provided by publisher.
Identifiers: LCCN 2024049683 (print) | LCCN 2024049684 (ebook) | ISBN 9798889896487 (lib. bdg.) | ISBN 9781682778142 (paperback) | ISBN 9798889897286 (ebook)
Subjects: LCSH: Ninja—Japan—History—Juvenile literature. | Ninjutsu—Juvenile literature. | Espionage—Japan—Juvenile literature. | Guerrilla warfare—Juvenile literature. | Hand-to-hand fighting, Oriental—Juvenile literature. | Martial arts—Japan—Juvenile literature.
Classification: LCC UB271.J3 G55 2026 (print) | LCC UB271.J3 (ebook) | DDC 355.30952—dc23/eng/20241213
LC record available at https://lccn.loc.gov/2024049683
LC ebook record available at https://lccn.loc.gov/2024049684

Printed in India

A ninja museum display

CONTENTS

Introduction **9**

Stealthy Start **13**

Pop Culture Ninjas 18

Ninja Guide 24

Tools of the Trade **29**

Walking on Eggshells 37

Ninja Weapon Museum 41

Ninja Moves **44**

Chirping Floors 49

Ninjutsu Skills 54

Famous Fighters **59**

Robin Hood Ninja 70

Female Ninjas 75

Selected Bibliography **76**

Glossary **77**

Websites **79**

Index **80**

Introduction

From the beginning of time, wherever groups of people have lived together, they have also fought amongst themselves. Some have fought for territory or control of basic necessities, such as food, water, and shelter. Others have been spurred to fight by religious differences. Still others have fought solely for sport. Throughout the ages, some fighters have taken up arms willingly. Others have been forced into battle. For all, however, the ultimate goal has always been victory.

OPPOSITE: Although the Japanese fighters called ninjas were primarily tasked with spying, they were trained for targeted killings, too.

OPPOSITE Ninjas were found on all sides of the chaotic wars between Japanese groups.

The warriors now known as ninjas emerged in medieval Japan during a time of intense fighting between families and **clans**. The infighting that was a hallmark of the Warring States Period (1467–1568 BCE) required that leaders gather information about their current and future enemies. Knowledge helped them to strategize about possible attacks as well as to prepare to defend themselves against strikes. To gather the information, they needed special forces. These forces were trained to secretly observe other groups, gather what they could, and destroy the enemies' resources. The spies were also often called upon to fight.

The earliest records refer to these exceptional Japanese spies as *shinobi*. Over time, they became known as ninjas. They passed on their skills from generation to generation and played a critical, although often secret, role in the wars between leaders in Japan. Eventually, they also helped bring the regional fighting to an end and to usher in a time of relative peace.

なら法師

Stealthy Start

During the 14th and 15th centuries, Japan was a dangerous place to be. The country was divided into provinces, all ruled by individual **warlords** who fought each other for land, wealth, and power. The warlords did not want to be ruled by the shogun, the commander of Japan's military. Instead, they created a **feudal system** of government and engaged in bloody civil wars that lasted for almost 200 years.

OPPOSITE: An illustration from the late 1700s of a ninja warrior and his weapons

Many battles were fought by foot soldiers and samurai warriors. Samurai were members of the elite, powerful warrior class in Japan. Their heroic efforts were well documented in stories and artwork. They were greatly respected for their strength and bravery and were often elevated to a high social status. But another group of warriors was quietly helping as well: the *shinobi*, also known as ninjas.

Ninjas were less visible than the samurai. They wore disguises and often operated under the cover of darkness. As a result, their exploits were less frequently documented in historical materials. But their reputation as stealthy secret agents became legendary in Japan. Many people associated ninjas with magic. They believed the spies were capable of passing through locked doors, walking on water, beckoning fire, and shape-shifting into birds and other animals.

In reality, ninjas were normal human beings—with a lot of specialized training. Many came from disadvantaged backgrounds and a lower societal class. They were not allowed to become samurai, who held higher positions in society as members of the aristocratic or warrior castes. Instead, ninjas trained under masters of the art of ninjutsu. The martial art strategy is based on secrecy, **espionage**, and unconventional warfare. The ninjas' **guerilla** tactics distinguished them from the samurai warriors, whose strict code of honor did not allow for such behavior.

OPPOSITE A photo of the last shogun, Tokugawa Yoshinobu, taken in 1867

During the shogun wars, ninjas acted as **mercenaries**. They were hired by daimyo, or feudal warlords, to spy on rival warlords. Their primary responsibility was to use disguises, stealth, and distraction to obtain secret information for their masters. Although ninjas carried weapons and were trained for battle, targeted killings were not usually their objective. Ninjas usually fought only to disarm their opponents, defend themselves, or to ensure that they would be able to deliver information and complete their missions.

In the 14th century, more than two dozen ninja schools existed in Japan. The schools focused on ninjutsu. The discipline may have been inspired by Chinese war strategist Sun Tzu (544–496 BCE), who many believe authored the influential military book *The Art of War*. The most prominent schools were located in the

The Tycoon of Japan

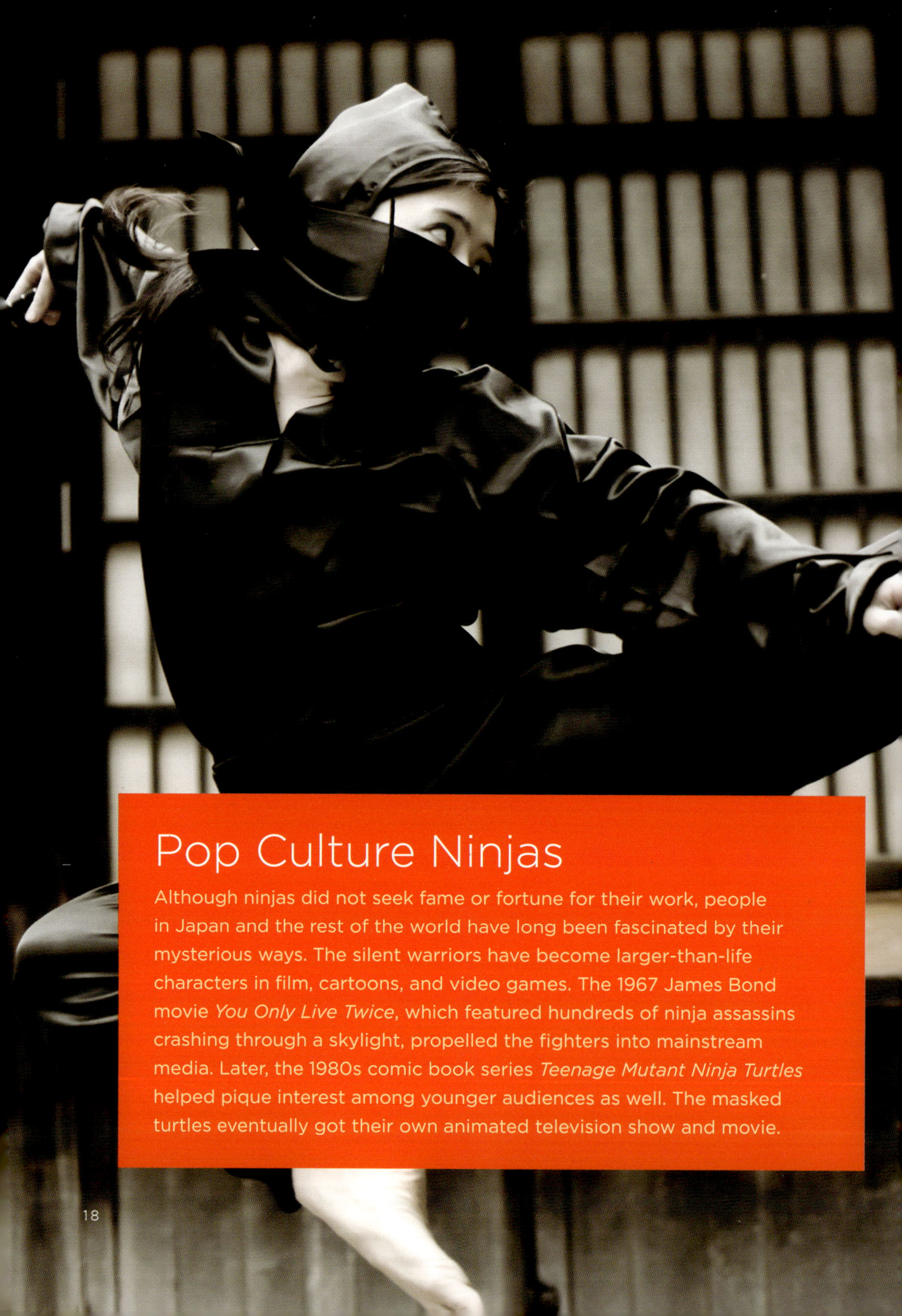

Pop Culture Ninjas

Although ninjas did not seek fame or fortune for their work, people in Japan and the rest of the world have long been fascinated by their mysterious ways. The silent warriors have become larger-than-life characters in film, cartoons, and video games. The 1967 James Bond movie *You Only Live Twice*, which featured hundreds of ninja assassins crashing through a skylight, propelled the fighters into mainstream media. Later, the 1980s comic book series *Teenage Mutant Ninja Turtles* helped pique interest among younger audiences as well. The masked turtles eventually got their own animated television show and movie.

mountainous provinces of Iga and Koga. Many of the most well-known ninjas trained there. However, ninjas from one province generally distrusted ninjas from another. Many Iga ninjas, for example, considered those from Koga to be rascals and frauds.

Ninja training started in infancy. Families conditioned their babies to be aware of everything around them. By the time children were five or six years old, they were playing games that emphasized balance and agility. They then progressed to rolling, jumping, and striking flexible poses. As teens, they practiced swimming and learned to breathe underwater using hollow bamboo poles. Some teens hung from trees for hours to learn patience or practiced silently leaping from tree to tree.

Although physical training was a necessary part of the ninja education, many lessons also focused on mental and social skills. Ninja students were taught how to use memory aids called mnemonic devices to help them recall information they discovered. For example, they might assign numbers or letters to specific body parts to trigger memories of enemy names, troop size, or other details. Students learned conversational skills so they could engage with different classes of society in various social settings. They studied astronomy. They learned how to prepare certain medicines and poisons. They practiced picking locks.

Ninjutsu training also addressed self-discipline and self-control. Ninjas were taught a series of 81 different hand gestures that were intended to help them stay focused and find inner strength during dangerous encounters. In addition to calming the ninjas, the hand positions were also meant to befuddle enemies. Some of the gestures were said to be hypnotic or capable of producing temporary paralysis, although there is no proof that such effects actually happened.

Most ninja operations were done in complete secrecy. Ninjas were rarely celebrated for their contributions to successful battles. Many were forbidden to speak of the roles they played, even to their own families. But they did do vital work and eventually helped Japan transition from a state of war to a time of peace.

Portrait of Oda Nobunaga

There are records indicating that squads of ninjas were often deployed to burn the castles of rival leaders. In 1558, for example, 48 ninjas were sent to burn Sawayama Castle, a military stronghold in the city of Hikone. The ninjas stole a lantern with the family crest of their enemy on it. They replicated that crest and created other lanterns, which they then used to get past the guards and gain entry to the castle. Once inside, they used the same lanterns to set fire to the structure.

Another example is the Honno-Ji incident. In 1582, a powerful shogun named Oda Nobunaga

Ninja Guide

One of the most comprehensive ninja guides was compiled by Fujibayashi Yasutake, a ninja master, in 1676: *The Bansenshukai.* Within its 22 volumes, *The Bansenshukai* describes how to achieve the "correct mind" of a ninja, craft disguises, and use the elaborate, often deadly tools of the trade. In 2013, *The Bansenshukai* was translated into English for the first time. The authors, Antony Cummins and Yoshie Minami, include a warning that readers should not try to re-enact or recreate the military tactics described in the book. The translation, they stress, should be used "for research purposes only."

had a plan to end the ongoing civil wars and unify Japan. He had the support of two other shoguns and several followers, but his plan was opposed by many warlords. Nobunaga was killed by a samurai general who also intended to kill Nobunaga's **allies**. Hattori Hanzo, a ninja from Iga, learned of the plot. With the help of other ninjas, he was able to protect Tokugawa Ieyasu, who also wanted to unify Japan. The ninjas worked together to help Ieyasu escape enemy territory and return safely to his home in Mikawa. When Japan's emperor made Ieyasu a shogun years later, in 1603, the country gradually entered a period of peace that lasted for two centuries. If ninjas hadn't saved Ieyasu, that may not have happened for many more years—or ever.

During the transition to peace, ninjas remained active in Japan. They served as castle guards and were hired to

OPPOSITE Tokugawa Ieyasu's appointment to shogun ushered in a time of peace in Japan.

assist on raids and sieges. But as the need for espionage and guerilla warfare decreased, ninjas used their skills in other ways. Some became security guards. Others used their training to become doctors, martial artists, or **pyrotechnics** experts.

Ninja traditions have continued in Japan, even though they are no longer an active part of the society. The stealthy warriors have become pop culture icons who are celebrated in books, television shows, and movies. Ninja toys and costumes are favorites among children. Ninjutsu skills are taught in martial arts classes around the world, and practitioners can easily find replica weapons online.

There is still a "ninja grandmaster" alive today who trained with descendants of the Iga and Koka ninjas in Japan. But in 2012, Jinichi Kwakami, the current grandmaster, said he would not appoint someone to take his place. "We now have guns, the Internet, and much better medicines," he said in an interview. "The art of ninjutsu has no place in the modern age."

Tools of the Trade

Ninjas considered their minds to be one of their most important tools. They had to be creative problem-solvers who could think fast during a mission. They had to be able to remember detailed information to pass on to their masters. They had to be mentally strong enough to face dangerous situations, knowing that their lives were always at risk. But ninjas weren't sent out on their missions with their minds alone. They were also outfitted with many specialized weapons to help them succeed.

OPPOSITE: Small swords called katanas were efficient, easy-to-carry weapons for ninjas.

Ninjas are often depicted wearing black, belted robes with black hoods and masks—a look that was first popularized in *You Only Live Twice*, a James Bond movie released in 1967. But in feudal Japan, ninjas wore disguises that mimicked the garb of everyday people. There were seven common characters that ninjas dressed as: merchants, priests, monks, farmers, acrobats, and musicians. In those recognizable outfits, ninjas could operate in broad daylight.

Disguises require more than the right clothes, though. In *The Bansenshukai*, 3 of the 22 volumes are devoted to operating **incognito**. They offer guidelines related to *shihogami*, or preparing one's hairstyle for different regions. They encourage ninjas to be fluent in the language and actions of whatever profession they are imitating. "If you try to impersonate the appearance or speech but have no skill in the trade, your stratagem will easily be revealed," the English translation says. "Therefore, you should learn in advance not only how to look or speak like the person you are going to impersonate, but also the art of the trade they do."

Within the folds of their disguises, ninjas often hid weapons that were compact, easily concealed, and deadly. One of the most common weapons they carried were *shuriken*, also

Skilled swordsmiths made katanas and other steel-bladed weapons by hand.

廣重画

known as throwing stars. *Shuriken* were small, star-shaped weapons made of iron. They had sharp points that could cause serious injury when thrown with great force at an opponent. Sometimes, *shuriken* were coated with poison or buried in dirt and animal waste to allow bacteria to build up on the surface. If a contaminated point cut deeply enough, the poison or bacteria would enter the victim's bloodstream and often lead to a fatal sickness.

Ninjas also carried small swords called katanas. Katanas, which were also the preferred weapon of samurai, had curved blades. They were roughly 24 inches (61 centimeters) and were usually worn across a ninja's back. That placement made it easier for ninjas to run and climb without worrying about their weapon. Ninjas had access to an assortment of other swords as well, including some that were shorter and easier to conceal, such as the *ninjato*.

If the mission called for it, ninjas carried blowguns—short, hollow tubes through which darts could be shot with a puff of air. Because the darts could be propelled from a short distance with a near-silent breath of air, victims were often taken by surprise when they were struck. And because the darts were usually coated in poison, that surprise was often followed by a quick death.

Depending on the circumstances, ninjas might also be armed with a short bow called a *hankyu*. Like the katana, the *hankyu* could be slung across a ninja's back while on a mission. With the bow, ninjas shot bamboo arrows called *ya*. Because of its diminutive size, the *hankyu* could not be counted on to hit distant targets, but it was very effective at close range. The arrows were often armed with explosives or flames so they could set wooden structures on fire. Some arrows, however, were designed specifically to make an eerie howling sound as they flew. The noise alone was sometimes enough to terrify enemies and send them running.

One of the ninja's simplest weapons was often one of the most effective: a long stick or staff called a *bo*. A full-length *bo* was approximately 6 feet (1.8 meters) long. Sometimes, a *hanbo*, or half stick, was used instead. A skilled ninja could wield either weapon to slash at or stab enemies

Walking on Eggshells

Smoke bombs were particularly important tools for a ninja. They could create a distraction, provide cover for escape, or temporarily blind the ninja's enemies. Often, those bombs were made out of eggshells. Ninjas would drill holes at the top and bottom of an egg, drain out the yolk, and then plug up one of the shell's holes with wax. They then added a combination of ash, gunpowder, and other chemicals to create the smokey effect they were hoping for. The eggshells were carefully tucked into a protective pouch, where they could be easily retrieved when needed.

or to deflect advancing opponents. A full-length *bo* was especially handy when battling multiple people at once.

One of the teachings in *The Bansenshukai* is to plan each mission carefully and carry only the essential weapons and tools needed for that particular mission. Tools that could serve multiple purposes were especially prized by ninjas. Iron claws, for example, were primarily used to help climb walls, but the curved finger hooks could also double as protection against sword attacks or be used to inflict a painful blow.

TOOLS THAT COULD SERVE MULTIPLE PURPOSES WERE ESPECIALLY PRIZED BY NINJAS.

Lengths of chain, known as *kusari fundo*, could be used to deflect a sword blow, to choke an opponent, or to sweep enemies off their feet. The *kyoketsu shoge*, which was a knife with a curved hook attached to an 18-foot (5.5-m) rope with a steel ring at the bottom, was especially adaptable. The hook and rope could be used to help climb walls and mountains. The knife could be used to attack. When thrown, the rope and ring could knock adversaries off their feet. In some cases, firecrackers could be tied to the steel ring and then be used to blind opponents.

A whole suite of weapons was designed to fit on a ninja's hand. The *shinobi shobo* was a precursor to modern-day brass knuckles. It featured a steel ring attached to a solid steel shape that could be hidden in the palm of a hand. Steel claws called *nekkote* slipped over a ninja's hand and fingers. They had knife-like claws that could cut enemies during hand-to-hand combat. Sometimes, those claws were dipped in poison to make them even more deadly. Such weapons were effective only if the ninja was able to reach the intended target.

Many tools were devised to help ensure safe passage through treacherous surroundings, such as steep mountains, rivers and forests, guarded gates, and fortress walls. Ninjas were prepared to use the supplies on hand to create rope ladders, floating bridges, rafts, and collapsible boats. They knew how to use hollow bamboo shoots to breathe underwater, sometimes for hours at a time. They carved

Ninja Weapon Museum

Although replicas of ninja tools and weapons are available through retail outlets, there are only a few places where real ninja artifacts can be seen. One of those places is the Ninja Weapon Museum in Kanazawa, Japan. Its collection includes approximately 160 artifacts, including several throwing stars, authentic armor, and other weapons. There are also replicas of katana swords and iron claws. As part of the museum experience, visitors can practice throwing replica *shuriken* at targets.

small wooden footprints that mimicked the paws of animals or children's feet and then attached them to the bottom of their shoes. These fake footprints covered the evidence of their own tracks and made it harder for enemies to follow.

Ninjas also had access to early James Bond-like gadgets to help them obtain information and gain access to secure spaces. They used listening devices, including the cone-shaped *saoto hikigane*, to **eavesdrop** on conversations behind closed doors. They had many tools for picking locks and entering buildings. They also used sharp picks known as *tsui giri* to create holes in walls

提燈

OPPOSITE An actor demonstrates how ninjas wore their weapons on their back.

through which they could spy on the inhabitants and assess the area before entering.

Ninjas sometimes used **incendiary** devices alongside their weapons. They made their own firecrackers, smoke bombs, and smoke pots. They learned how to work with gunpowder to create tools that would distract enemies and provide cover for secret activities. Sometimes, fire was also used as a deadly weapon. Ninjas often destroyed enemy strongholds with fire or used firecrackers and flaming weapons to blind their opponents.

Ninja Moves

Ninjas practiced the traditional martial art of ninjutsu. Martial arts are systems of combat that originated primarily in Japan but were common in other Asian cultures as well. They were designed for military training and self-defense. In addition to the physical training, there was often a spiritual component. Martial arts were seen as a lifelong practice focused on centering the body, mind, and soul.

There are 18 different skills traditionally associated with ninjutsu. Like other forms of martial arts, such as karate and judo, ninjutsu training includes both unarmed and armed combat. Specific classes of weapons receive special attention. Because a ninja's primary duty was to spy, their training focused on stealth and disguises.

It was important for ninjas to develop superior strength to prepare for extreme conditions and changing circumstances. Mountain running was a common training technique for building strength, speed, and better lung capacity. According to some records, ninjas could run between 30 and 125 miles (48–201 kilometers) a day. They were expected to maintain a weight of approximately 132 pounds (60 kilograms), so they could be fast, nimble, and light on their feet.

To be stealthy, ninjas had to be able to move as quietly as possible. They learned to walk on the outsides of their feet, on tiptoe, and on their heels—all techniques to conceal sound. To avoid detection, they also stepped by moving their right arm and leg at the same time, followed by the left. Silence was so critical that before a mission, ninjas were made to walk on a sheet of wrinkled Japanese paper called *washi*. If they made a single sound, they were most likely pulled from the operation. Ninjas also stayed lower to the ground by bending their knees while walking. That made it harder for guards to spot them than if they were standing tall.

Ninjas also had to be careful about any odors that might alert guards to their presence. They did not smoke or eat spicy foods. Those smells could be carried on their bodies and clothing and be detected as they snuck into a building. They kept themselves clean and were said to take frequent **herbal** baths to reduce the risk of body odor that would give them away to their enemies.

Ninjas planned around the weather, the cycles of the moon, and the **topography** of the region when mapping out a mission. They wanted to move in the opposite direction of the wind, to reduce the possibility that sounds and smells would reach their target before they did. They needed to know when the moon would be brightest so they could plan their route outside the path of its light. They looked for elevated areas that would allow them to watch their target from all sides.

Ninjas were taught to carefully observe their surroundings and to make decisions based on what they saw. For example, they watched birds flying overhead. If the birds suddenly changed the direction in which they were flying, that might indicate that people were nearby. But if many birds were flying freely around a castle, that meant that there weren't many guards in position. Ninjas made weather predictions based on the dewdrops on spiderwebs, rings around the moon, and the twinkling of the stars.

Chirping Floors

Ninjas had to be especially careful of "nightingale floors," which made birdlike chirping sounds when stepped on. The floors were made of dry wood planks, anchored by nails. The nails rubbed against a fastener when pressure was put on the wooden planks. The chirping sound they made alerted guards and residents to an intruder's presence. Ninjas had to learn to avoid nightingale floors or to walk on them without being heard. No one is sure whether the chirping floors were intentional or just a result of the building materials available at the time.

須磨 十二
豊国画
佐野喜

OPPOSITE Few fighters in history moved and completed missions as quietly as ninjas.

Although rain made some missions more difficult, it also hid the sound of footsteps as ninjas approached a target.

Once inside a castle, ninjas had to be prepared to hide if necessary. Before entering, they often had a plan for where to seek shelter—in a big pot, for example, or in a loft space or stable. If they came upon a guard, they would move as close to a wall, tree, or fence as possible and stand completely still, with their back to the enemy. They held their breath, or breathed as silently as possible, until the guard left. Another option was to assume the "quail hiding" position, in which the ninjas pulled in their arms and legs, crouched down, and tucked in their head, face down. In both cases, they may have silently chanted a hiding spell called *ongyo* as added protection.

When ninjas were required to fight, either as part of their mission or because they were caught, they often engaged in *taijutsu*, or unarmed combat. They were trained to use chokeholds, leg sweeps, and other **grappling** techniques, as well as punching, kicking, and blocking moves.

To punch, ninjas used several hand and fist formations, including an extended-knuckle fist known as *shikan-ken*. In this formation, the fingers were half folded, with the middle knuckles protruding. The ninja used the fist to punch with force straight at a target—often an enemy's face, breastbone, or ribs. Ninjas also used *shuto*, or sword hand, to strike with the curved outside edge of the palm on an opponent's neck, limbs, or joints.

Ninjas learned both offensive and defensive positions. These moves allowed them to react quickly to an enemy's advances and to be prepared to block a strike or absorb a hit safely. *Taijutsu* training included break-falls that minimized injury, evasive rolls, and deflective leaps. Often, those moves were followed by a series of kicks and punches.

On many missions, ninjas would have nothing but their *bo* to use as a weapon. Their *bojutsu* training prepared them to use a variety of spins, slashes, and blocks to battle an adversary. Those moves were paired with special body movements to build power and force behind the stick. Ninjas practiced daily to become proficient in figure-eight spins, downward-smash strikes, and overhead, side, and low blocks.

Ninjutsu Skills

Ninja training, or ninjutsu, encompassed 18 different martial art skills. Although the application of those skills varied from school to school, many common threads existed. Together, they supplied a ninja with mental, physical, espionage, and battle training.

Seishinteki kyōyō—spritual refinement
Taijutsu—unarmed combat
Kenjutsu—sword techniques
Bojutsu—stick and staff techniques
Sōjutsu—spear techniques
Naginatajutsu—pole weapon techniques
Kusarigamajutsu—sickle-and-chain weapon techniques
Shurikenjutsu—throwing weapons techniques
Kayakujutsu—pyrotechnics
Hensōjutsu—disguise and impersonation
Shinobi-iri—stealth and entering methods
Bajutsu—horsemanship
Sui-ren—water training
Bōryaku—tactics
Chōhō—espionage
Intonjutsu—escaping and concealment
Tenmon—meteorology
Chi-mon—geography
Hojojutsu—rope techniques

The movements taught in *kenjutsu*, or sword techniques, were similar to those in *bojutsu*. Ninjas were taught several basic cutting movements, blocking movements, and attitudes, or positions, to use during a fight. Swords were used to cut diagonally from the hip to the shoulder or the shoulder to the hip; horizontally across the body or downward across the head and face; and in a thrusting motion. Ninjas knew how to attack the vulnerable areas of an enemy's body and would look for opportunities to target the hands, wrists, legs, and arms.

Sometimes the ninja's most effective moves involved strategic deceptions rather than weapons. Some stories say that ninjas would carry a fake love letter with them when they entered a castle or large residence. If they were caught, they would pretend that they were only there to deliver the message to a maid. Or they would try to

WHEN ESCAPE WAS THE ONLY OPTION, NINJAS WERE TRAINED TO DO SO IN A WAY THAT WOULD CAUSE CONFUSION OR DESTRUCTION.

distract enemies by yelling directions to a non-existent ninja, to create confusion and encourage them to chase after someone else.

When escape was the only option, ninjas were trained to do so in a way that would cause confusion or destruction. One tactic involved throwing a stone or other object in the opposite direction or, when possible, into nearby water, in an effort to throw off pursuers. Another was for the ninja to yell loudly, as if they were one of the pursuers themselves. When armed with firecrackers,

A variety of *shuriken*

ninjas could light them to distract enemies and allow extra time to get away. And when it appeared that a ninja was close to being caught by a single pursuer, they could drop down on bended knee and allow the enemy to crash into them—giving the ninja time to attack and get away.

Famous Fighters

The nature of their work meant that few ninjas identified themselves publicly. The secrecy of their missions was critical to their success, so most ninjas and their deeds remained unnamed and unknown to almost everyone. However, over time, stories have been told about a few ninjas whose feats of bravery and successful missions made them legendary warriors in Japan.

OPPOSITE: Hattori Hanzo was a highly skilled ninja whose successful missions helped unify Japan.

Perhaps the most famous ninja is Hattori Hanzo. Hanzo was born in 1542 into the samurai class. Although he was born in Mikawa, his family was from Iga, which is known for ninjas, not samurais. Hanzo returned to Iga as a young boy and started training as a ninja when he was about eight years old. He went on his first mission, to Udo Castle (also called Uto Castle) on the island of Kyushu, when he was between 15 and 16 years old. He led a group of ninjas over the wall and into the castle and helped defeat the guards. His skill in fighting at Udo Castle led the shogun Tokugawa Ieyasu to give him the nickname "Demon Hanzo."

After that, Hanzo served Ieyasu. At about age 20, he led a group of ninjas on a mission to rescue the shogun's daughters, who had been captured and taken to Kaminogo Castle by the rival Imagawa clan. In 1582, he became

Elaborate Japanese castles often served as the homes of warlords.

OPPOSITE Unlike Hattori Hanzo, most ninjas remain faceless shadows to history.

most famous for saving Ieyasu's life from a murderous enemy. Hanzo not only protected Ieyasu, but he also smuggled him through both Iga and Koga provinces to find safety in Mikawa. Ieyasu went on to become a leader in Japan who helped lay the groundwork for the eventual unification of the country.

Hanzo was a leader of the Iga ninja clan and helped trained hundreds of ninjas. He was only 55 years old when he died in 1596, following an illness, but his legacy continued long after his death. Hanzo has been celebrated in many movies and **manga**. His physical strength is often complimented by such magical powers as the ability to move objects with his mind, see the future, and vanish into thin air.

Like Hanzo, Fujibayashi Nagato trained in Iga. He became a leader of the Iga ninjas during the 16th century.

A page from *The Bansenshukai*

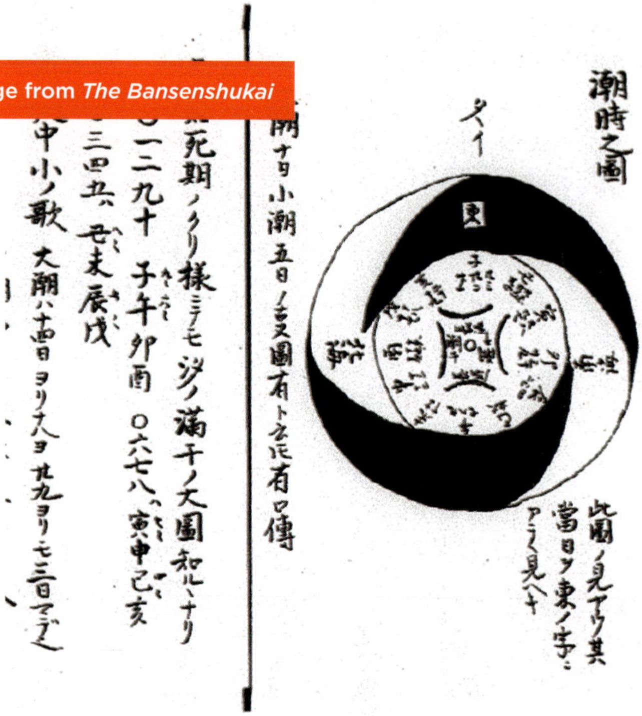

He served a daimyo named Oomi, who was intent on defeating his rival, Oda Nobunaga. Nagato's ninjas were so persistent that Nobunaga tried to eliminate the ninja clans from both Iga and Koga, invading the provinces in 1581. Although Nobunaga's warriors killed many people and left a path of destruction in their wake, they were

ALTHOUGH NOBUNAGA'S WARRIORS KILLED MANY PEOPLE AND LEFT A PATH OF DESTRUCTION IN THEIR WAKE, THEY WERE UNSUCCESSFUL IN WIPING OUT THE NINJAS ENTIRELY.

unsuccessful in wiping out the ninjas entirely. Many ninjas went into hiding, both to protect themselves and to ensure that their way of life would continue.

Years later, one of Nagato's descendants, Fujibayashi Yasutake, is believed to have further preserved ninja culture. He documented the ninja lifestyle and required training in *The Bansenshukai*, which is now known as the Ninja Encyclopedia.

Momochi Sandayu is considered one of the three greatest ninjas of all time, alongside Hanzo and Nagato. He led the Iga ninjas during the second half of the 16th century. He was rumored to have split his time between three different homes, with three different families, to protect his identity as a ninja.

Like Nagato, Sandayu frequently battled Oda Nobunaga. Some stories suggest that he died during Nobunaga's invasion of Iga and Koga in 1581. One of his homes was burned down during the invasion, leading to speculation that he didn't survive. Other stories insist that Sandayu escaped, gave up the life of a ninja, and settled down as a farmer in Kii province. However, his grave was reportedly discovered in 1960, not far from one of his homes in Iga. The truth of what happened to Sandayu, like most of his life as a ninja, remains a mystery.

OPPOSITE Female ninjas were rare but highly effective, as few men suspected traditionally clad women as spies.

Fuma Kotaro did not train in Iga nor lead ninjas there. His clan was based in the Sagami province, which was known more for horsemanship and naval warfare. The ninjas that Kotaro led—some reports say he commanded a band of 200—had a reputation for being pirates and burglars who caused chaos and left destruction in their wake.

A once-popular story said Kotaro killed fellow ninja Hattori Hanzo by burning his boats with oil. However, that version of events has since been dismissed as fiction. The circumstances of Kotaro's own death are more certain. He was caught by Tokugawa Ieyasu's special law enforcement team in 1603 and beheaded.

In Japan's **patriarchal** society, most ninjas were men. But stories exist of at least one legendary female ninja: Mochizuki Chiyome. She was married to Mochizuki Nobumasa, a samurai warrior who was killed in battle in 1561. When

Robin Hood Ninja

Although most ninjas were paid to steal secrets and fight rivals, the legend of Ishikawa Goemon makes him sound more like medieval Robin Hood than a Japanese warrior. Goemon was said to have used his ninjutsu skills to steal riches from the wealthy. He then shared that bounty with poor peasants in hopes of making their lives easier. Legend has it that Goemon was caught trying to kill a powerful warlord and was executed by being boiled alive in a vat of oil. Although that gruesome end is documented in artistic renderings, no one is sure whether the story of Ishikawa Goemon is fact or fiction.

五右衛門
一勇斎国芳画

her husband died, Chiyome went to live with his uncle, a powerful warlord named Takeda Shingen. Shingen knew that Chiyome's family was from the Koga clan, which meant that she had ninja roots. Shingen needed ninjas to help him gain more territory and defeat neighboring warlords. He encouraged Chiyome not only to practice ninjutsu herself but also to recruit and train a band of female ninjas to work for him. Chiyome was so successful in building her army that Shingen won many battles and gained great power in the region before dying in 1573.

Although ninjas have not been officially active for many centuries, some of the traditional ninja clans have tried to keep the culture alive. The once-divided provinces of Iga and Koga have combined as the Koga Ban clan, and Jinichi Kawakami serves as the last head of the family. Kawakami, who was born in 1949, began studying ninjutsu when he was six years old. He learned the traditional methods of combat and espionage. He taught the traditions to other students as well. Now in his 70s, Kawakami has said that he will no longer teach ninja skills to others, in part because those skills have become irrelevant in the modern world. Also, students would not be able to practice true ninjutsu practices without being arrested. That is why many call Kawakami "the last ninja."

The moniker "the last ninja" may seem misleading to some. There are many academies and schools around the world that continue to teach ninja skills. Training videos are easily accessible online as well. But although many of those are legitimate martial arts centers that provide good training, they are not connected directly to the ninjutsu traditions that began in Japan or to the original **bloodlines** of the ninja clans.

Some people argue that ninjas continue to exist just as secretly as they did in the 14th and 15th centuries. More likely, however, today's ninja warriors exist only in movies, video games, and comic books. Either way, the legacy of their traditions lives on, and the fascination with their stealth and strength will continue as well.

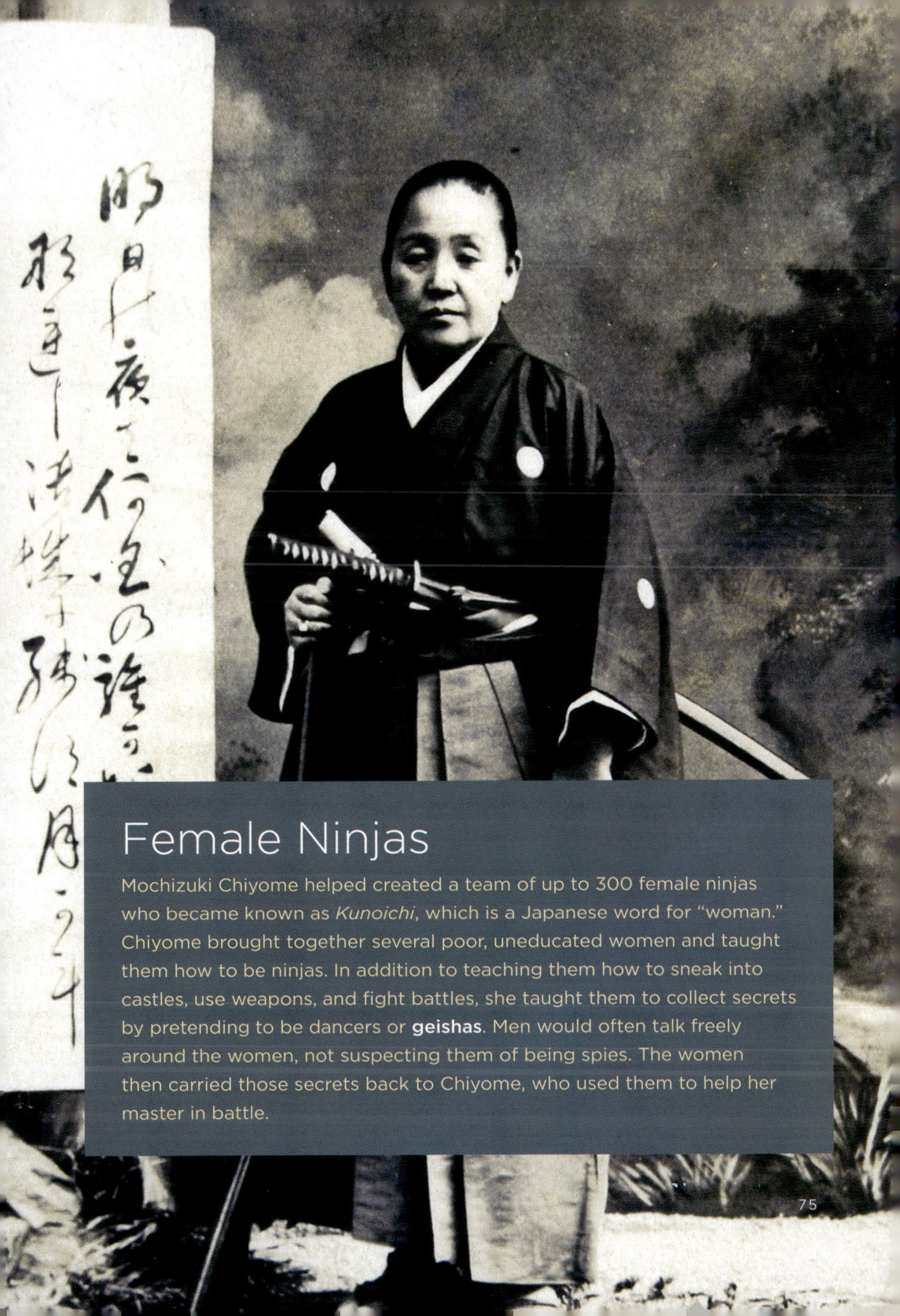

Female Ninjas

Mochizuki Chiyome helped created a team of up to 300 female ninjas who became known as *Kunoichi*, which is a Japanese word for "woman." Chiyome brought together several poor, uneducated women and taught them how to be ninjas. In addition to teaching them how to sneak into castles, use weapons, and fight battles, she taught them to collect secrets by pretending to be dancers or **geishas**. Men would often talk freely around the women, not suspecting them of being spies. The women then carried those secrets back to Chiyome, who used them to help her master in battle.

Selected Bibliography

Fujibayashi, Yasutake. *The Book of Ninja: The First Complete Translation of the Bansenshukai, Japan's Premier Ninja Manual.* Translated by Antony Cummins and Yoshie Minami. London: Watkins Publishing, 2013.

Hayes, Stephen K. *The Ninja and Their Secret Fighting Art.* Rutland, Vt.: C. E. Tuttle Co.: 1981.

Kim, Jeanhee. "Ninjas: How Japanese Spies Evolved into Pop Culture Heroes." History. November 10, 2023. https://www.history.com/news/ninja-history-shinobi-feudal-japan.

Man, John. *Ninja: 1,000 Years of the Shadow Warrior.* New York: William Morrow, 2013.

Szczepanski, Kallie. "The History of Japanese Ninjas: Feudal Warriors Who Practiced Ninjutsu." ThoughtCo. July 17, 2019. https://www.thoughtco.com/history-of-the-ninja-195811.

Turnbull, Stephen. *Ninja: The Unofficial Secret Manual.* New York: Thames & Hudson, 2019.

Glossary

ally	a person or group that cooperates with another; a friend
bloodline	a person's family history that is connected by blood
clan	a group of people united by family, location, or common interest
eavesdrop	to secretly listen to a conversation
espionage	the practice of spying or using spies to obtain information
feudal system	a political, social, and military system based on the relationships between landowners and workers
geisha	a Japanese woman trained to entertain men by talking, singing, and dancing
grappling	fighting without weapons
guerilla	relating to activities performed in an unusual way, often without authorization
herbal	made with aromatic, medicinal, or savory plants called herbs
incendiary	designed to start fires

incognito	with one's identity concealed, sometimes by using disguises or false information
manga	a genre of Japanese comic books and graphic novels
mercenary	someone hired to fight for someone else
patriarchal	relating to systems that are controlled by men
pyrotechnics	the art of making and displaying fireworks
topography	the physical features of an area, such as hills, valleys, and waterways
warlord	a military commander who governs alone

Websites

Ninja

https://www.worldhistory.org/Ninja
Find out more about ninja costumes and martial arts training.

Ninja Facts for Kids

https://kids.kiddle.co/Ninja
Learn about ninja history and view a weapons gallery.

Ninja Weapon Museum

https://www.ninjaweaponmuseum.jp
Discover images of common ninja weapons.

Index

assassinations, 9, 16
The Bansenshukai, 24, 30, 38, 65
books, 24, 26
Chiyome, Mochizuki, 69, 72, 75
clothing, 30, 47
daimyo. *See* warlords
disguises, 24, 30, 31, 45
distractions, 16, 37, 43, 55–56
female ninjas, 69, 72, 75
Goemon, Ishikawa, 70
hand gestures, 20–21
Hanzo, Hattori, 25, 59, 60, 63, 66, 69
hiding position, 51
Honno-Ji incident, 23
Ieyasu, Tokugawa, 25, 26, 60, 63, 69
Imagawa clan, 60
Japan
  Iga province, 19, 25, 26, 60, 63, 64, 66, 69, 72
  Koga province, 19, 26, 63, 64, 66, 72
  Sagami province, 69
Kaminogo Castle, 60
Kawakami, Jinichi, 72–73
Kotaro, Fuma, 69
Kunoichi, 75
Kwakami, Jinichi, 26–27
language skills, 30–31
magical powers, 15, 63
mission planning, 47–48, 51
movement, 45–47, 49, 51
  without odors, 47
  without sound, 46–47, 49, 51
movies, 18, 26, 30, 63, 74
Nagato, Fujibayashi, 63–64, 65, 66
nightingale floors, 49
ninja grandmasters, 26–27
ninja schools, 16, 19, 54, 73
Ninja Weapon Museum, 41
ninjutsu, 15, 16, 20, 26, 27, 44, 45, 52, 53, 54, 70, 72, 73, 74
  bojutsu, 53, 54, 55
  kenjutsu, 54, 55
  taijutsu. *See* unarmed combat
Nobumasa, Mochizuki, 69
Nobunaga, Oda, 22, 23, 25, 64, 66
observation skills, 10, 48
Oomi, 64
samurai, 14, 15, 25, 35, 60, 69
Sandayu, Momochi, 66
Sawayama Castle, 23
shihogami, 30
Shingen, Takeda, 72
shoguns, 13, 16, 23, 25, 26, 60
spying, 9, 10, 15, 16, 26, 45, 75
television shows, 18, 26
tools, 38–39, 40–41
  iron claws, 38, 41
  kusari fundo, 39
  kyoketsu shoge, 39
training, 10, 15, 16, 19–20, 26, 44, 45, 60, 63, 72, 73, 74, 75
Tzu, Sun, 16
Udo Castle, 60
unarmed combat, 45, 52–53, 54
warlords, 13, 25, 61, 64, 70, 72
Warring States Period, 10
weapons, 16, 23, 26, 29, 31, 32, 34–36, 38, 39–40, 41, 43, 45, 53, 54, 55, 56–57, 75
  blowguns, 35
  bo, 36, 38, 53
  fire, 23, 36, 43
  firecrackers, 39, 43, 56–57
  hanbo, 36
  hankyu, 35–36
  katanas, 29, 32, 34–35, 36, 41
  nekkote, 40
  ninjato, 35
  shinobi shobo, 39–40
  shuriken (throwing stars), 31, 34, 41, 57
  smoke bombs, 37, 43
  swords, 29, 32, 34, 35, 38, 39, 41, 54, 55
  ya, 36
Yasutake, Fujibayashi, 24, 65
Yoshinobu, Tokugawa, 16